See the Bike

by Cameron Grieft
illustrated by Anthony Lewis

Practice Decodable 5

McGraw Hill Education

Bothell, WA • Chicago, IL • Columbus, OH • New York, NY

MHEonline.com

Send all inquiries to:
McGraw-Hill Education
8787 Orion Place
Columbus, OH 43240

ISBN: 978-0-02-145973-5
MHID: 0-02-145973-8

Printed in China

8 9 10 11 12 DSS 27 26 25 24 23

A  is on a .

boy bike

A 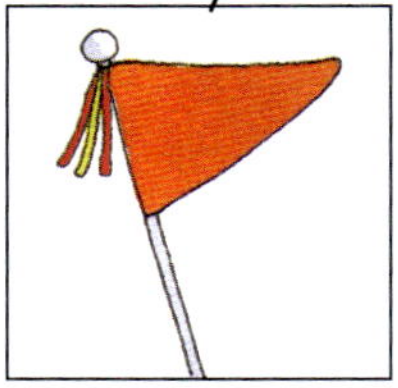 is on the .

flag bike

I can see the 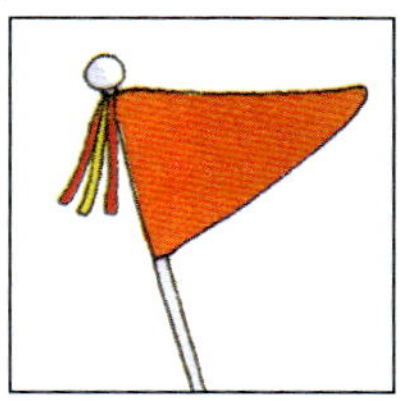 .

flag

The  bike is on the  hill.

I can see the 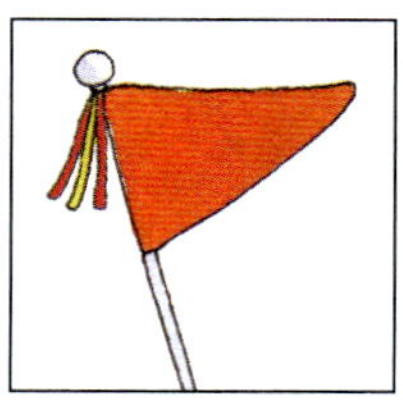.

flag

I can see the  there.

bike

I can see the 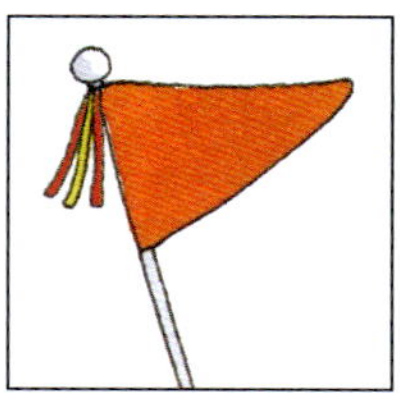 flag on the  bike.